Paula's Praise

From Defeat to Victory

Paula Geoghegan

Paula's Praise: *From Defeat to Victory*

by Paula Geoghegan

Copyright pending 2025

(Front cover photo is of Paula and her mother. Her father is in the background. Both her parents are deceased.)

(Back cover photos are of Paula's paintings: the Treasure Box, the Park Scene, and the Praying Hands for the World)

ISBN 978-1-961482-16-6

Dedication

I dedicate this book to my heritage, my children: my son Paul, my daughter JenNel, and my son Joseph; my granddaughter Faithe and my great-granddaughter Nevaeh; my grandsons John and Jacob; my brothers and their families; my sister and her family; my aunts and uncles and their families; and all the generations to come.

I want to show my heartfelt gratitude and special thanks to all the Pastors and Wives (listed individually below) for all their dedication, prayers, and sacrifice they gave for me and my family. It is greatly appreciated.

There is a song of dedication to all of you; it is by Ray Boltz. It is called "Thank You." The lyrics include: "Thank you for giving to the Lord. I am a life that was changed...."

> To Pastor and Sister Mark Huba
> To Pastor and Sister Ed Lawson
> To Pastor and Sister Janet Elsworth
> To Pastor and Sister Phillip Johnson
> To Pastor and Sister Bobby Bell
> To Pastor and Sister Dwight Taylor
> To Pastor and Sister Eric Sierra
> To Pastor and Sister Maurice Rodriquez
> To Pastor and Sister Larry Jenkins

Thank you for your service to the Lord in bringing the Word of God to my family and myself. Thank you for being Godly men and women of Excellence. Each one of you are vessels of Honor, and truly showed me the Love of Jesus.

And to each wife, you have taught me prayer, kindness, teaching, and the list could go on and on. Thank you for all the wonderful things you have done.

Sister Paula Geoghegan

Table of Contents

Foreword by Peggy L. Jenkins

Introduction

Autobiography

Foreword

"Forgiveness is for me—I can only find forgiveness when I give forgiveness." (David Michael Brown)

Through childhood abuse, sexual assault, and husband infidelity, Sister Paula Geoghegan (goHAYgun) has survived by the grace of God—because He knew she would seek Him until she was filled and satisfied in and with the pureness and power to be an overcomer. In her darkest moments outside of Christ, Sister Paula sought to know God. It was that dedication of seeking and diligence of surrendering that brought her joy, unspeakable joy, in the Lord.

Her joy is complete in Jesus. Thus, He can trust her—and has trusted her liberally—with insight into various situations of life. And because of her desire to see others saved (others who might be suffering similarly to her experience) she is led to give her praise on pages written for those co-sufferers who can be comforted by the same Comforter she knows so well.

Meet the Comforting Christ in Sister Paula's Praise.

Peggy L. Jenkins Author of Frush's Journals

Introduction

"When I talk about outings we were taken on, and how at Christmas, great-grandmom would make a beautiful Christmas village under the tree with lights and cars and street lights (it looked like something from Thomas Kincaid), as a kid, I would smile and feel safe with them. They could only take us to their house once in a while, but it was always something to hope for. And they would fill our bellies with food."

You are probably wondering, since I had such a dysfunctional childhood, why I'm talking about outings. Well, when you are a young child and you walk into a home and your father is beating up your mom and then running after the kids, and there's no food to eat because his addiction made him spend his hard-earned money on liquor, you don't want to remember the abuse. You want to remember the good.

Everyone in life has a story, a background. As I take you on this journey of my life, I hope you too will see how the Lord was instrumental in placing people in our lives to help and give us hope.

Autobiography

Hello. My name is Paula and I want to take you on a journey of my life. I was one of five children. I have three brothers and one sister: Jerry, Tim, Paula, Ron, and Sue.[1] My father and mother struggled like any family. Mom stayed home while dad worked. My father had an addiction to alcohol that cost him his marriage. My mom tried to cope, but his erratic behavior took its toll on all of us. I am happy to say, late in his life he stopped drinking and was a good productive man.

I remember my father's violent behavior, and always living in worry and fear as how he would come home from his over-the-road truck driving events. When he was sober, he was okay. But my childhood was far from normal, and very dysfunctional.

My brother Tim instilled in himself good values, and went to college. And Jerry always protected us. He became a businessman. Ron learned from my grandfather who taught him mechanical things; he is a genius and can build just about anything. My sister has worked, has great insight and is very knowledgeable. I am happy to say my great-grandmom's, grandmom's, and mom's prayers prevailed. All of my siblings have wonderful families. The good Lord kept His hand upon our lives, and now I can look back and see that.

Oh, but you say, how is that, if there was so much violence and dysfunction? Well, the moment people start to ask God for help and prayer, He steps in. You may not see the results immediately, but know this one thing: God is a prayer-answering God.

My great-grandma and my mom's mom (who we called Nany) lived close by each other around the block, and I knew they prayed for us. My great-grandma lived near a convent, and she would prepare a pot of soup for the nuns and have one of us kids deliver it to them. I always remembered them touching my head. Now, I wonder how many people prayed for us, and I thank God for His guardian angels.

---

1 These names have been changed to protect their privacy.

Visiting great-grandmom's house

My great-grandmom and great-grampa would pick us up in their Falcon car; my brothers and sister would be so excited because we knew this was our outlet, our refuge, and safe house. They would put us in the car and drive to the bakery so they could buy fresh-from-the-oven rolls. Then they would take us to the "auction." Here in Florida, we would call it a flea market. And there they would go to the Italian deli and buy knockerwishes. (It's like a big fat garlic hotdog.) They kept a jar of mustard in the glove box. Then they would take us to the park where we would eat the sandwiches and play on the playground. Then we went off to the auction.

There my great-grandma would buy boiled peanuts. All of us kids would be eating the peanuts and walking, meanwhile leaving a trail in the dirt until we got to the entrance. Then they walked us until great-grandma would find a little village house to add to her Christmas village collection. Great-grandpa would get a tool or an item. She would get a little something for each of us, then when we were done, she would say, "Okay, everyone in the car." And they would drive home. When we arrived, she would say, "Play with the toys in the toy box. I have to make dinner." Then she would fill our bellies. I remember for dessert she would give each of us a tray filled with hostess cakes, curly corns, and soda.

After dinner, each of us got a bath, and then we were told to get PJs on. Sometimes, she would play Candyland, Pick-up-Stix, and Password. Then she would read to us and just talk to us. Or she would tell us that we would have to go home the next morning. All of us would be quiet because we enjoyed both of our grandparents. They played cards with us, and taught us structure and good memories.

When I talk about outings we were taken on, and how at Christmas, great-grandmom would make a beautiful Christmas village under the tree with lights and cars and street lights (it looked like something from Thomas Kincaid), as a kid, I would smile and feel safe with them. They could only take us to their house once in a while, but it was always something to hope for. And they would fill our bellies with food.

Nany who lived on the next block was my mom's mom. She cooked a lot of Italian meals. She had a front porch where we could play games or just sit and talk.

My mom was a good mom. She would make clothes for us, and she would try, but with five children and a drinking husband, it was a load. I could never understand why all this happened: the abuse my mom had taken, the yelling, the black eyes, the bruises, us kids not having food, and him even going after us.

As the violence got worse, a neighbor told us of a church that could send a young person to bring us kids to church. We went only a couple of times, then the church got a bus. The first time we got on the bus, there was only one sibling with me. The bus driver said, "If you come next week and bring some others, you can stick your hand in a penny jar for each person." So, the next week I brought my brothers and sister. I got to stick my hand in the penny jar four times, and I loaded my little purse and thought, "We won't go hungry tonight!"

We all went into the church service, and I sat next to a man in a wheelchair. They were passing around this plate. I asked the man next to me, "What is that for?" He said, "Offerings." I said, "What is that?" He said, "Money for God." I asked, "Is He broke?" He laughed and said, "It's to pay bills and to buy Sunday school books." When the plate got to me, I set it on my lap and dumped all of those pennies in the offering plate, and boy! Did it make a lot of noise! Then the man said, "The Lord bless you" and he patted me on my head.

You are probably wondering, since I had such a dysfunctional childhood, why I'm talking about outings. Well, when you are a young child and you walk into a home and your father is beating up your mom and then running after the kids, and there's no food to eat because his addiction made him spend his hard-earned money on liquor, you don't want to remember the abuse. You want to remember the good.

But it wasn't until late in my life that I could see the hand of God. Even though we only went to church a handful of times, I remembered things. I remembered my great-grandmom and great-grandpop and Nany telling us they were praying for us.
Hope…Shattered

In the midst of this violent atmosphere, we moved away from New Jersey where all my mom's family lived. We moved to Florida. My father had gotten a contractor license after simply reading a book on construction (he was very knowledgeable), and there he built a beautiful home for us. For a brief time, it seemed like things were going to change… except I guess the pressure of five children and a wife and a contracting business got to be too much, and he went back to drinking. The violence started again.

I remember being outside at midnight, sitting under a street light with my dog, and the neighbor calling me a whore and all sorts of evil things. And all I could say to myself was, "Is my mom okay?" I felt such guilt, like I had let her down. He would give her blackeyes, and if we were in the way, he would toss us too, so I would run.
Be a Virgin

My mom would tell me, "Be a virgin until you get married." Then it was 1968.

I was walking home from school one day, and it was raining really hard. My father's work friend asked me if he could take me home. Little did I know that home is not where he would take me. He took me to his place of business, and molested and raped me, and he told me if I ever told, he would hurt me. This would and did continue for some time.

We had a neighbor who was a real nice lady. She used to help my mom. She asked my mom if everything was all right with me; she noticed I was quieter and more withdrawn. My mom and dad didn't know this man was hurting me. You see, I was only nine.

One day the lady stopped me because she had noticed the man's car at the bus stop. She must have had a sixth sense something wasn't right. Though he told me I would be sorry for telling anyone, she asked me and kept asking until one day I told her.

She confronted him. The next thing I knew, she was injured in a bad accident.

After that, a couple of my friends and I were sitting on the hood of a car. The two girls were in bathing suits and I was in long pants. This same man whom I feared jumped into the car (it was his, a different car he'd purchased which I didn't recognize). He sped off and I slid off because of my slick pants on the hood (whereas my two friends in bathing suits didn't budge). I was screaming and sliding, and when I slid off onto the ground, somehow he ran over my leg.

He stopped the car; the two girls sat there in shock. I half-sat, half-laid in the road in pain for several minutes, feeling my leg. All the skin was moving. I was so scared, yet none of them moved to help me or answer my call, "Help me!"

Finally, he picked me up and put me in the backseat and drove to the hospital. That's where he left me. A security guard carried me inside. I saw the guard's shirt all bloody, and kept saying, "I'm sorry."

My mom finally arrived, and when my dad showed up, the doctor said they couldn't save my leg. I remember my dad yelling, "You better, or I am going to kill that man!" (My mom and dad were still unaware of the ongoing assault.)

All that kept going through my mind was, "Did he do this on purpose? Will I lose my leg?"

Finally, after many months of physical therapy and skin grafting and repairing bones, my leg looked like I'd been in a fire. I was so distraught, so sensitive. I kept thinking as I went from a wheelchair to a cane, "I never want anyone to see my leg."

Still, none of my family knew what that man had done to me before the accident. Out of fear, I never mentioned it when we went to court that followed concerning the accident. But that ended the sexual abuse from my abuser.

Nearly Drowning

About a year later, my mom took all of us to the beach. I wouldn't wear a bathing suit because of the scars on my leg, so I went swimming with my pants on. When I tried swimming further out along with my brothers, the pants began to drag me under. I was literally drowning when my little brother saw me and saved me.

Becoming aware of my anxieties about the appearance of my leg, Ron kept telling me, "Don't worry about what others say or think." But other than family, no one knew or understood the source of my fears and insecurities.

As time went on, I went from a nine-year-old girl to a girl who didn't like herself. I felt I let my mom down, suffering guilt when she was abused. And I didn't understand why I had this ugly leg, even though the sexual abuse had stopped.

My mom must have sensed I was insecure. She made stylish school dresses for me, but even with that, I was still unhappy. I kept thinking the only men I could trust were my brothers.

Our Family Splits

My mom finally had had enough of the violence. She planned to leave, but financially could only take my two younger siblings with her: my sister and youngest brother. (My second brother had already gone to live with my aunt and uncle.)

When she left the house for her flight back to New Jersey (while my dad was at work), she could only wave and tearfully tell me she was sorry. I anxiously thought in my ten-year-old mind, "Oh, now what's going to happen next?"

That night my dad was drinking and yelling and blaming my mom for leaving, and I guess I had had enough. I picked up and chucked a liquor bottle, busting a China cabinet there. Then I took a second bottle of liquor and began to pour it down the sink, saying, "This is why she left!" It was his last bit of liquor.

In his unreasonable anger, he grabbed me and was choking me when my oldest brother jumped on his back and I fell to the ground. Dad turned on him, and my brother took the beating.

I was so frustrated, so angry, I just wanted someone to help us. When my dad was sober, he was good. He would take us camping, and to the beach, but I just couldn't understand as a kid, nor help him regarding the addiction and his actions.

A Change for Me

The Good Lord heard the prayers of my mom and her family, and intervened. The next day my father said quietly, "I better send you to your mom."

I believe from him seeing what he did to me and my brother, he realized he had hurt both of us. I think from me standing up to him, and his wife leaving, and him losing his family, things might have been showing him that liquor was taking him further than he wanted.

A few days later, he made arrangements for me to fly to New Jersey, and I knew I was returning to the grandparents who could and would help. But concerned, all I kept thinking was, Is my brother going to be all right?

When he took me to the airport and we were pulling up, my brother and I were in complete silence. When we walked in the door, my dad simply repeated, "I think I better send you with your mom."

I remember flying in the plane to see my mom, and knowing I was going to her, the one who I knew loved me; the one who came to the hospital when I had been run over, and who comforted me.

In New Jersey

In New Jersey, we started going to a Nazarene church of a friend of my mom. Even my mom went, but all she did was cry. Then she didn't go any more. She still wanted us to go, but we weren't regular attenders.

After two or three years, my oldest brother moved to be with us. He helped my mom by getting a job; he was fourteen. Things were a lot different. We went to school; we were near our grandmothers, and they were a good influence on us. I remember my grandpa grew a beautiful vegetable garden. It was amazing the work he put into it.

Turning Eighteen

My dad and my mom had gotten a divorce, and eventually they both married other people. When I turned 18, I went to live with my great grandmom. I worked at a factory and seemed to have a more peaceful life. When I got laid off my job, I decided to visit my younger brother, Ron, who had moved to Florida, married, and had a baby daughter. After that visit, I decided to move back to Florida. I had my own apartment. I worked in a factory during the day, and at night I cleaned City Hall. And on every other weekend, I would serve for a catering service. I enjoyed going to the beach and Tarpon Springs sponge docks, and going to nice restaurants. It seemed I had a busy but peaceful life.

Then I met a man who became my first husband. Initially he kept trying to date me, but I had been heartbroken so I kept brushing him off. He was persistent…he brought me huge stuffed animals, flowers, and well… I finally agreed. We dated for a short time before marrying. He was 6'6"and weighed 350 pounds. I guess I was looking for someone who could protect me. I'll call him Don.

I paid for the beautiful wedding which many of our families and friends attended. We started out good because I had an apartment and furniture, and Don had a van. We both worked at the same factory; he worked nights and I worked days. But early in our marriage, Don was always having his buddy over. Don was soon addicted to drugs, and all-day hours of video games. Then he wasn't working at all. We argued: I told him if he wasn't going to work, we weren't going to stay together. I was going to get a divorce.

Chapter 1 - Anger and Bitterness: Divorce

Even when the bills began to pile up, Don still didn't believe me. After I had to sell a lot of stuff to pay bills, I thought, "I am over this!" I finally went to a lawyer and easily got a divorce.

After the divorce, Don went to the preacher who had married us and told him I divorced him. We got this preacher out of the phonebook because neither one of us were going to church. The preacher asked what happened, and when he heard Don wasn't working, he told Don he understood why. I guess the preacher gave him a scripture about a man who won't provide for his family, and explained the rest of the scripture, that it's worse than denying the faith.

"But if any provide not for his own, and specifically for those of his own house, he hath denied the faith, and is worse than an infidel" (I Timothy 5:8).

Don tried coming back, but I said, "Not until you prove you will work."

Meanwhile I left the apartment and moved in with Jerry (my oldest brother), his wife, and their daughter, who were new believers. They watched a lot of Christian TV. I remember a preacher was asking if you want Jesus in your life, because if your life hasn't gone well, "You can say this sinner's prayer." So, I did.

While I was staying at my brother's, they took me to a church where the pastor was a reformed biker. I don't even know what he preached about, but he was walking toward me and saying that I had a call on my life, and he wanted to pray over me. I remember saying, "Mister, don't touch me!" My family indicated it would be okay, but I said, "It's not okay with me!" Remembering my past experiences, I was uncomfortable around men, and I didn't yet understand the things of God.

A short while after that, Jerry saw in a newspaper that another church was having a tent revival. When he said, "Let's go!" I asked, "What is that?" He said, "A church service in a tent."

My little niece and I, and Jerry and his wife, all got into his van and we went. We pulled into the parking lot, and a man greeted us at the van and said, "Welcome! We have been praying for people to come." We walked into the tent and sat down, the only white family there. All of a sudden, they were playing loud music and jumping. Uncomfortable, I got up to leave, and that man stood at the door of the tent and said, "We've been praying. Don't go!" Well, I wasn't going to argue in that tent, but I sure was not understanding anything that was going on. Then it seemed to get really loud. They were calling for people to go up front.

Jerry and his wife went up front, and my niece and I watched them. Suddenly, I saw sparks over people's heads (an indication, I learned since, of the presence of the Holy Ghost). I kept blinking my eyes, and I asked my niece if she could see what I saw. She said, "Yes, I see them too!" By this time, I was ready to run out, but that same man was standing at the door. I was worried, and not sure what to make of all this.

After a short time, the music stopped and then the preaching started. I don't even know what he preached, but I thought, "Is Jerry and his wife okay?" They were smiling and happy. My niece and I were very quiet on the ride back to the house. You see, fear of the unknown is intimidating.

After all of this, Don kept trying to get back to me, so I finally said he had to work. Jerry got him a Mack truck, but Don only drove it around with his old buddy. Then Jerry gave him a job, and we remarried. Soon after, I got pregnant. I didn't know it, thinking I merely could not have children after my past experience. But I passed out while working where I cleaned apartments. A visit to the doctor revealed the truth.

Don changed jobs then, and began to work as a wrecker driver. He seemed to like that.

Soon after, I received an inheritance from my great-grandmom. Jerry took me to Tennessee where I bought a little store and garage. (I had wanted to purchase a house rather than the store-and-garage, but Don said he would run a wrecker business from the garage until we could get on our feet. I shouldn't have listened!)

On a second trip there, Don and I learned that the Tennessee neighbors were very kind; they came to the property with sickles to cut down the tall grasses. They told me of their harsh winters. Because I was pregnant, I told Don I would not stay if he couldn't hold a job, because on the side of that mountain, I couldn't be without power. (When I was without power in Florida—because of an unpaid bill—at least I could live out of a cooler.) We stayed in Tennessee just a couple of days and came back home.

Returning from Tennessee after the first trip

When Jerry and his wife dropped me off at my apartment—we returned a day early—I put my key in and opened the door. There was my husband in bed with a woman!

Though Don was saying she was homeless, and I was answering, "I don't care!", I gathered all her stuff and put it in a trash bag, opened the door, and tossed it out. Little did I know that my father-in-law was at the door, and the bag hit him. I felt terrible because I really liked him. The girl went running out.

My father-in-law asked what was going on. I yelled, "Ask your son." He continued to ask me questions. I told him I didn't want Don to have women friends, but he clearly could see the situation.

I'm so glad he showed up, as the situation got defused. But Don and I became distant following that.

Paul's Birth

In hard labor in the hospital with a midwife present, I kept telling

Don something was wrong. After thirty hours of labor, a doctor was called and finally delivered the baby. It was difficult as the cord was wrapped around the baby's neck, and they struggled to revive him. I heard Don yelling, "Save them both!"

I remember floating above my body then, and seeing them trying to revive me. They worked a few minutes, then when I opened my eyes, I saw Don holding Paul. Later, they asked me questions that if I were truly unconscious (without the experience of floating above and watching events), I never could have answered. But to their amazement, I was able to answer, having seen and experienced it all. Don kept saying, "I am just glad you're still here with me."

The next day, the hospital wanted us to go to a dinner for all the families that had a new baby. I kept saying, "I don't want to go." Because of the severe labor, blood vessels in my eyes had broken and it looked like I had two black eyes. Don encouraged me to go, so I did. But I felt the people there were saying, "You see that lady. Look at her black eyes." The look of an abused woman!

After we went home, because of the many stitches, I was in a lot of pain. Unbelievably, Don's ex-wife dropped off her young daughter, saying the little girl was going to stay with us. So here I was with a newborn and a five-year-old who didn't like me. And everyone saying they are glad I am alive, and I am saying, I just want to rest! Life was challenging. Though Don enjoyed holding our new son (this baby had personality plus! Everyone liked him, and he was very smart), this made his daughter jealous, and I was really concerned for the baby's safety.

A couple of months later I became pregnant again. Don began working for my two brothers who had started an asphalt company. About six months later, he claimed the heat was too much so he quit work. I was pregnant with our daughter, JenNel.

More Infidelity and Meeting Sandy

One day my sister-in-law, Don's older sister, came to my house to inform me that Don was in a bar with a woman, and I needed to take care of it. I told her I was eight months pregnant, and I couldn't do anything about it. After she left, I got on the floor in my house, and was praying and crying because I was so heartbroken. I was telling the Lord I couldn't fix Don, so could the Lord fix me.

There was a knock at the door just as I was asking the Lord what to do and for Him to help me. And I asked, "Who's there?"

"I'm Sandy, and I met you through our neighbor next door," I heard a voice say. "Wait a minute!" I called to her.

I composed myself, wiped the tears, and splashed water on my face, then opened the door. There stood a lady with a soft, gentle demeanor, and she said to me that as she was ironing that morning, a still, small voice told her to invite me to church. I asked her if she was a Jehovah Witness. She said no, a Pentecostal. I told her, "I don't even know what that is, but I was praying and asking God to show me what to do.

My husband's lifestyle is drugs, drinking, and women." I told her what I asked God to do: "I can't fix him, so fix me."

She said, "Come to church with me on Sunday." I agreed to follow her there.

When I married Don, I thought he wouldn't let anyone harm me. Little did I know that through his running around, he would break my heart. When Sunday came around, I got my son and myself dressed. We were going to follow her when she said, "Let me drive you." I agreed, and we got in her car.

As we arrived at the church, I saw all these women and men in dresses and suits, and I was already feeling out of place. Being pregnant, my emotions were off the charts. We went in and I sat down and held the baby; I was scared. I was in my blue jeans and felt awkward.

Then I looked up as the music began to play. Some people were crying—tears running down their faces—and others were running, some were dancing, and one behind me was whooping and hollering. I had never seen this before except at the tent revival. They say fear of the unknown is intimidating. I must have had a look of puzzled confusion when suddenly an elderly woman sat next to me and whispered in my ear, "Don't leave! The Lord brought you here!" I stayed and listened to the preacher, but thought the woman could read my mind because I was thinking if I had my car, I would have left.

I stayed through the whole service. I don't remember what he preached, but it brought a sense of peace, even goosebumps on my arms from his teaching from the Word of God. I felt great peace in that place, and furthermore could sense it from the smiles on the faces.

Chapter 2 - Getting a Bible Study on Baptism

I didn't go back to church for a while, but Sandy invited me to her Home Interiors party. Members hold home parties, and sell pictures, shelves, candles, and much more. I said I would come. I was wondering why this nice lady was being kind to me, to invite me into her home with all these godly-looking ladies. I had been smoking three packs of cigarettes a day, so I wasn't sure if they would like me. However, they were very kind to me.

After we had some food, one of the ladies (Lori Lanigan) asked me if I would like a Bible study. I said, "Okay," but that I didn't know much about the Bible. I only saw it "just sitting on a coffee table.... I don't know much about church or God, but I pray to Him." She asked me if I thought the Bible was God's Word, and I said "Yes." She said she would set it up.

Sister Lanigan gave me a home Bible study called "Into His Marvelous Light." And as she expounded on the Word of God, things made sense to me. When she showed me the scriptures about being baptized and receiving the Holy Ghost (as stated in Acts 2:38), I said I should get baptized because it is something the Lord wants us to do.

When I was baptized the following Sunday, I experienced a lightness that had little to do with my eight-months' pregnancy; I felt the fulfillment of a longing that only Jesus can fill. I had walked the Salvation Road of Acts 2:37-39:

Now when they heard this, they were pricked in their heart, and said unto Peter and to the rest of the apostles, Men and brethren, what shall we do? Then Peter said unto them, Repent, and be baptized every one of you in the name of Jesus Christ for the remission of sins, and you shall receive the gift of the Holy Ghost. For the promise is unto you, and to your children, and to all that are afar off, even as many as the Lord our God shall call.

That day, I invited Sandy to come eat at my home after the service. While I made lunch in the kitchen, from the couch where she was sitting, Sandy saw a woman in a bathing suit coming from a room in my house. She called me out of the kitchen, and asked me who that was. I looked out the patio door and said, "That is my backdoor neighbor."

Again, I felt such brokenness.

Sandy said she had to go call the pastor, knowing what I had to face with my husband's continual and ongoing unfaithfulness.

Baby Shower

Sister Rebecca Huba and the ladies of the New Port Richey church then gave me a beautiful baby shower. None of my family came; they didn't understand this new faith connection. I remember walking into the shower in the church basement, and crying because I had so many beautiful gifts, a display of their love. The people showered me with cards and words of encouragement, and loved me. I was absolutely in awe of the blessings and love and kindness they showed me.

I had my daughter, JenNel, in November. It was 1988. (Paul had been born in October, 1987.)

Weeks passed into December, and I was hoping for this "present" from God which they called the Holy Ghost. I was still too frightened to have anyone pray over me or touch me. I told the Lord if He wanted me to receive the experience, that He could do it.

Chapter 3 - Receiving the Holy Ghost

It was a Sunday, and the Pastor told me if I would come to the communion service that night (it was New Year's Eve), I would get this Gift: the experience of being filled with the Holy Ghost evidenced by speaking in other tongues. I had learned about it at the Bible study, and even read about it in the Book of Acts. He said I would see people receive it.

Still, I was a little skeptical and nervous. I had seen people speak in another language, and then they would glow and shine like they were illuminated. I wanted that Gift these people had. I couldn't believe the God who made the heavens and the earth wanted me to obey His command to Repent (turn from my sin), and to be baptized in the name of Jesus where He would remit my sins. I had to make it a priority.

Don's family was coming over on New Year's Eve for their party. Beforehand, I cooked the ham, and made the potato salad, and all kinds of food all day. Then I bathed my children and put them to bed and said I was going to church.

Don strongly objected! I said, "Yes, I am going. I was told I am getting a Gift from God."

He laughed and I said, "I did everything you need, now I want to go!" He stood in front of the door and demanded that I stay home.
I looked up to heaven and said, "I don't know what to do." Then suddenly his father walked over and said, "Let her go and don't question the things of God."

I went to church while my husband's family was bringing in the New Year with their alcohol. But I was determined to get to church to receive this Gift.

When I arrived, the preacher taught about communion and foot washing. When it came time for the foot washing, an elderly lady said to me, "Will you wash my feet?" I said, "I never did this before." She said, "As you are washing my feet, just pray and talk to the Lord."

The next thing I knew, I was on the floor, speaking in an unknown tongue and praising God. I knew the Lord had done something special in my life. And I got the promised rest. (See Isaiah 28:11-12 For with stammering lips and another tongue will he speak to this people. To whom he said, This is the rest wherewith ye may cause the weary to rest; and this is the refreshing....)

After this feeling of being on Cloud Nine, I found peaceful inspiration in painting. I began to create pictures of stairways to heaven, painting doves in flight, and creating all sorts of expressions of heavenly scenes—using scriptures in each.

Infidelity Continues and its Results

Meanwhile Don was still cheating. The backdoor neighbor's husband—after finding them together in his house—came to my door, saying, "If they are getting together, why don't we?" I told him if he didn't leave, I was calling the law.

That night I told Don about the visitor, and he simply made light of it. I was so hurt, so sad. Later that night, he went out drinking as usual.

Because Don wasn't paying the bills, we were going to be evicted. I was overwhelmed. Suddenly the woman he was cheating with came in my back door and nearly collapsed at my feet where I was washing dishes. She was hysterically crying, saying her husband was leaving her. Meanwhile she looked at me and said, "I destroyed your marriage and hurt you!"

I thought to myself, I could hurt her...but then I wouldn't have my children.

Then I heard the Lord's still, small voice speaking to me, telling me to give this woman my ring: my crucifixion ring. It was my favorite ring because I would look at it and think of Jesus. God's ways are not our ways, and I couldn't grasp it all; I just knew to obey.

I took it off my finger—maybe a bit reluctantly—and handed it to her. I told her to "Trust in Jesus no matter what you go through, and He will be your Answer."

Chapter 4 - Entertaining an Angel

After that we moved from that house. The Lord provided money (an inheritance) and we bought a beautiful home…and I was going to church. My pastor's wife was teaching me a foundational Bible Study. I went to four of the fourteen lessons before we moved again, and I couldn't get to church. But the Lord kept trying to connect me with people…and we would move again.

"I don't know how to serve You or what You require," I told the Lord. And because I needed to stay in church, I didn't understand my identity in Christ. I wasn't building my faith by hearing the Word of God as in Romans 10:17 (So then faith cometh by hearing, and hearing by the word of God). So I drifted away.

One day I was in a buffet restaurant with my two children and Don. My children were restless, and he was barking orders. "Go get me a piece of pie now!" I was unhappily thinking in my mind, "He is always angry! I wish things were different." The children were affected by the troubling spirit between us.

When I went up for the pie, an elderly man was standing behind me and he said, "Hey lady, do you want to hear a joke?" I asked him if it was clean. When he said yes, I said okay.

He said, "Do you know why Adam and Eve were not able to raise Cain? Because they weren't Able without God!"

I knew enough about the story of Cain and Abel, and Adam and Eve their parents who fell from grace. Though it was a play on words, it spoke to me that without God, I can't do anything. I realized I couldn't do anything without God or by myself. I felt the Lord had just given me the answer for which I was searching.

I turned around and the man was gone! I looked for him in the restaurant but I couldn't find him. My husband called loudly to me, and asked me what I was doing. I said, "Looking for the elderly man who told me a story. He was behind me."

Don argued angrily, "There was no one behind you!" I tried to describe the man, but Don wouldn't believe me.

I remembered that occasion all these years later as I write this. But I'm reminded of the Scriptures where it lets us know, we could be entertaining angels unaware.

Be not forgetful to entertain strangers: for thereby some have entertained angels unawares (Hebrews 13:2).

Anger and Bitterness

One night at 2 A.M., Don told me that I and the children had to leave the apartment because he was bringing his girlfriend in there, a woman he had met in a convenience store. I was very hurt because he chose this younger woman over me.

We started arguing loudly, and someone called the police. They learned that my name was not on the apartment lease, and they were making me pack my bags and the children's stuff to leave. I was crying; my youngest Joseph was only one month old; Paul was six years, and JenNel was five.

The police kept asking me if I could call someone. I called the Pastor's wife, Sister Elsworth. She said, "Don't go anywhere." I told her the police were escorting me out, so she said to put them on the phone. The police agreed to wait until she and her husband arrived. Don was calling his girlfriend to come over at the same time. He didn't know anything that was happening with me. When he asked what was the delay, the police told him they were waiting for the pastor and his wife to arrive. Then my husband said, "No, no! I'll let her stay the night."

Meanwhile, Pastor and Sister Elsworth arrived. When she walked into the room, the scene shifted as she took authority. She looked Don in the eye, and he was halted in his tracks. He turned to his girlfriend who had arrived, and they fled! The power of God was strong in the room. He left that night, and I remember praying deeply, "Not my will but Yours. And if You could let this pass from me, do so." In the morning, I knew I would be homeless. My emotions were wild. Then there was a knock at my door, and this elderly woman was standing there. She said, "I know you don't know me, but I heard all the commotion and I want to help you."

I said, "I am going to be homeless tomorrow." She said, "You and your children can come stay with me for a week. But I need help." I said, "What is it you need?" She said, "I don't have any furniture." I told her I wasn't allowed to take anything from my apartment. She said, "That's okay. I need you to help me get furniture."

I called the pastor's wife, and she told me where I could get furniture for free. With my six-year-old son Paul, I put furniture in the woman's van. She was happy, and I had a place I could stay temporarily. (I didn't have to go there; God had other plans.)

That day, as Don moved his girlfriend in, I realized it would be too traumatic to stay nearby with this elderly woman after what followed: I had thrown my wedding ring at Don, and the girlfriend had picked it up and kept it. She sneered at my daughter JenNel, and said that she would never see her daddy again; she was going to marry him.

That same day I stopped at the convenience store, not knowing the girlfriend worked there. As I faced her, I shouted, "I'm glad you're behind a bulletproof glass! You can rip my heart out, but when you hurt my kids, that's another story!"

I went to the lady's house where I could stay, and told her, "I can't stay. I think I would get into trouble, seeing my husband and his girlfriend." She told me to call my pastor's wife. I said, "I feel bad. I have not gone to the church much." She said, "Please!"

When I called Sister Elsworth, she told me to meet her at the church. I said, "I don't know where I am going to go, or what I am going to do." I had learned that she ministered to the homeless. She had great compassion, and showed it in her actions.

I met Sister Elsworth at the church. She let us in, and said the Lord spoke to her: the best thing she could do for me was teach me to let God intercede through me.

I have always just prayed, talking naturally to the Lord, but she encouraged me, saying, "God is going to give you the "gift of intercession,"--praying in an unknown tongue while you intercede for people and situations." She said I was going to need to rely on the Lord.

I poured out my heart then, and while we were praying, I felt deeply moved to speak in a heavenly language, a profoundly stirring language. When I was done, she gave me a sum of money for gas, and she prayed for me once again.

The Blue Couch and the Voice of God

Putting the baby in his car seat and the other kids in seatbelts, we set out to I didn't know where. I drove down Drew Street and saw a blue fur couch with mirrors on the side that looked like my great grandmom's, only hers was black. It had a free sign on it. I took that as my grandmom was watching over me. My six-year-old Paul looked at me questioningly; he asked, "Why are we getting a couch when we don't even have a home?"

It wasn't dirty or abused, so I said "Just help me get it on the roof of the car." With tears in my eyes and deep anger and hurt in my heart, I said to myself, "I don't know what I am doing." I couldn't tell my children. They were scared. So was I.

I went down the street, praying, "God, I don't know what I am going to do."

I heard the Lord say, "Call your oldest brother." I said, "Jerry is getting a divorce. He has enough troubles, and his wife has the trailer park." (In the divorce which had finalized, she received the trailer park for the income.)

I finally submitted to the Lord's prompting, and when I called, he said, "Sis, I only own one small trailer in there, but it is really bad, and I can't go in there."

I pushed. "Can you ask her if I can use the trailer? Otherwise, it's either the trailer or the car." He knew I was desperate. I was driving with the couch on the top of the car, and was teary-eyed.

"Stay at the phone booth, and I'll have to call you back," he instructed me.

When he called me back, he said I could use the trailer. It was just an RV trailer, but it would provide some shelter, and we had a couch! When we arrived, we observed the porch roof falling in and the other work—a lot of work—that needed done. It was really scary.

My niece (Jerry's daughter) and her half-sister were staying across the street. That afternoon, she brought a baby pool from the store, and watched the two older kids swim. While I cleaned with the cleaning supplies they gave me, they also watched the baby in the playpen. I really went to work. The sisters had some paint, and I painted, and used old towels and sheets to make curtains. I cleaned the old blue couch I had picked up and it became my kids' bed. The baby had his playpen; he was only a month old. I had to get help from the government for formula and other items.

We made the RV trailer our home. I still didn't go to church, but I knew the Lord had His hand on my children and me.

Daily Violence

Staying there was scary because a lot of people lived there who used

Paula Geoghegan

heavy drugs in the park. Once my niece came over to visit, and we were sitting in the living room when the Lord spoke to me and said, "Put your kids and your niece on the floor, and cover them."

It didn't make sense, but I kept feeling to do it as I learned to recognize the voice of the Lord, so I did. In seconds, the drug dealers in the neighborhood had a shootout, and they hit my trailer and a couple of others. It was frightening, but we were spared!

My niece said, "Don't tell my dad! He has enough stress! He will make us all move!" We had no place else to go, so we stayed.

One day after that, my step-niece's boyfriend (Jules) was running after her with barbells in his hand, raised like he was going to throw it at her. He'd been abusive, and was out to hurt her once more. Quickly, I told another niece to watch my kids and I ran outside and began to yell at him like a woman in distress filled with anger!

He had never had anyone pursue him before, and it frightened him! He ran away and locked himself in his car, and shakily tried to reassure me that he wouldn't hurt her anymore. He knew I was in a rage. This big bruiser, major drug dealer had never had anyone stand up to him.

Well, I'm lucky I didn't go to jail. I don't know what happened. I just had had enough.

The next morning this guy said to me, "I'll buy you something." Knowingly, I said, "You are not going to beat on me like you do on my niece, to keep me quiet!"

Following that, all his friends stayed away from me. That was a truly dark time in my life. I was bitter over the break-up of my marriage. I was angry all the time, and I lived somewhere that wasn't safe.

Another day I ran to the store while my same niece kept my three children. When I returned, Paul was gone! I asked frantically,

Paula's Praise: *From Defeat to Victory*

"Where is Paul?"

"I let him go with Jules, and they'll be right back," my niece responded as she tried to calm me down. I turned and took the other two kids home.

Meanwhile, I was anxiously looking out my window, doing dishes, and saw Paul and Jules return. Paul went to the backyard, and Jules followed him. When I looked, Jules had a gun pointed at Paul's head. (Later, Paul said Jules threatened that if he ever told where they'd gone, he would kill him.)

When I saw the gun, I went running after him with a heavy tool from my porch—which happened to be located there—screaming out of the desperation of a mother! He ran down the road to his fancy car, jumped in and locked the car. I climbed on the roof and threatened him with the heavy tool I was still grasping. He begged me not to hurt him. Friends of his—their gold necklaces around their necks—gathered from the neighborhood, hopping out of their cars to watch the action! I think he was more scared than I…, and he was the one with the loaded gun!

I realized we had to move.

Moving from the Trailer Park

We were finally approved to move into the low-income housing projects. When they showed me the place, I thought it was nice but I could see men who were living there with women, and they had fancy cars. I thought, This structure of apartment is nice, but it's the same type of neighborhood we are in, only a little nicer.

33

Chapter 5 - Restoration Back to Church

I remember walking up the steps and being noticeably out of breath because I smoked three packs of cigarettes a day from stress. I weighed about 105 pounds and looked like I hadn't slept in a long time. (Proverbs 13:15. Good understanding giveth favour, but the way of a transgressor is hard.) I was living in Hudson, and I heard the Lord say, "Go back to church...to the Pentecostal church."

My sister-in-law was planning a deliverance meeting at the Baptist church, inviting Pentecostal preachers and other denominational preachers to preach. She invited me. I wasn't going to go, but she was the one who let me live in the trailer park. So I went.

A Pentecostal preacher, speaking as a chosen guest at the Baptist church who had never met me before, spoke life into me during that service. He finished the sermon, then came down from the platform and walked up to me where I was sitting. He told me things only God knew. He said I didn't trust men, but the Lord wanted to teach me and heal me. He added that the man I was married to and had the children with had broken my heart, and that God wanted to heal the fractured pieces.

He asked if he could pray for me. And he prayed for my children, and for me. He didn't know how the Lord used him to speak words of life into my broken-hearted soul.

A couple of weeks went by. That same sister-in-law asked me to cook for a funeral dinner at the Pentecostal church which had lost a member that passed away. I agreed to cook a turkey with the fixings on one condition. I said, "If you take it to them."

What I didn't know was that this was the church where the Pentecostal preacher who prayed for me about my broken heart pastored: Pastor Johnson.

At the Beach

The Lord spoke to me about going to that little Pentecostal church, and told me my drinking buddies would not be around if I would give my life to the Lord.

One day I took my kids to the beach, and, as usual, I was drinking. That little Pentecostal church congregation was there, playing music on guitars, and other instruments. I remember having some money, so I thought, If you want me to give to that church, I will.

No sooner did I think that than a lady came over, and I gave her my money. She said, "I've seen you before."

"It was at the Baptist church where your Pastor preached," I said.

She said she was going to get the preacher. She told me his name: Pastor Johnson. I said, "That's not necessary."

Pastor Johnson came over and asked me if I wanted prayer. I said "No," but JenNel said, "You need to pray for her. My mom drinks." I objected, "You can pray for my children, but not for me."

Then suddenly the church people surrounded us. I felt overwhelmed. When they finished praying, JenNel said, "I want to be baptized."

"You are too young," I said.

"I'll baptize her at church on Sunday, and you'll come," Pastor Johnson gently instructed.

I said obstinately, "I won't go," and with humble conviction, he said, "Yes, you will." And I did.

Sunday came, and JenNel was baptized. I didn't bring her back, and we didn't return…for a while.

Everywhere we went it seemed, I would see these (church) people, and they would say, "We're praying for you!" I said, "I have had the best people pray for me, and I still didn't get it right." I was under conviction.

One lady said, "I am going to continue to pray for you." And sure enough I kept hearing the Lord say, "Go to that church." And I would say, "But I smoke, and I drink, and I am angry…." And He said, "Just trust Me. Do it for your children."

I finally went to church. I remember thinking as they had altar call, "I don't know how to change or quit smoking or give You all the hurt I have." God said, "Just go to the altar." I went, and as I prayed, He said, "Let Me help you with your life."

Well, that day, the Lord started working on me about my bitterness, and my nicotine addiction, and healing the hurts. When I finally surrendered, my life changed.

Listening to that Still, Small Voice

December came, and I didn't have enough money for Christmas gifts. I was sitting at my table, saying, What am I going to do? Then a still, small voice said, Look out the window. There is a man getting ready to throw out real branches from his Christmas tree. Ask him for them.

I asked the man, and he gave them to me. I went back in the house and said, It doesn't make sense to me unless You want me to make a wreath. He said, I want you to get out what little Christmas ornaments you have, and get the Bible. And I want

you to give your testimony. On each ornament I attached a scripture verse. I completed the wreath, using the ornaments.

God said, I want you to take it to Holy Ground Homeless Shelter, and drop it off. I learned this lesson: Little is much when God is in it.

I dropped off the wreath at the Shelter where a man took it and said, "Hey, Merry Christmas!"

"Merry Christmas to you too," I said, and drove away.

That night a little while later, I got a knock on the door and thought, Who could that be on Christmas Eve, so late? I answered the door, and saw the Director of Holy Ground Homeless Shelter standing there.

"How did you know where I lived?" I asked her.

She answered, "Everyone knows "the lady in the projects who goes to church." She just had to ask which apartment.

She said that of those at Holy Ground who read my testimony about the wreath, it brought a lot of them to tears. Touched, they prayed and wanted to do something nice for my children and me. They filled a huge black bag with clothes, shoes, and toys.

I remember crying and telling them the Lord used them as an answer to my prayer. I asked them whatever I couldn't use, could I share with some of my neighbors? She said, go ahead. I said, "Do you want me to wrap the gifts and say they are from you?" She answered, "Do however you feel."

I learned that day that when the Lord wants you to do things, then you should obey His voice, even if it doesn't make sense because He knows all things.

Many Awesome Things

That evening, I gave some toys to neighbors and we thanked Jesus for His blessings. Then that began my journey of learning to listen to the Lord's voice. After that Christmas and every year, the Holy Ground Homeless Shelter started distributing toys, clothes, and blessings of food into that neighborhood. They would often park in front of my house.

Our children were also blessed by the Lord through the Christian Motorcycle Club, and Quilter Guild. The churches helped, giving of their time and their talents to these children, so, even though they lived in a low-income housing project, the Lord shined on them and they received blessings in many ways.

I was known as the mom who had her doors open and children were allowed to come over to play video games, board games, or just for some juice and a safe place to be.

And out my back door was the swing set where children were always welcome. I would listen for the Lord to tell me what to do: pray for people, take children to church, take groceries to some, witness to others. I began to learn His voice.

One day a neighbor asked me if I could get my preacher to come pray in her apartment. Pastor Johnson was known as the strong "prayerful preacher," and I was known as the prayer lady who did Bible studies. The Lord was showing me many awesome things.

If you live in an unsafe place, you face many dangers each day. Wherever you live, may you look to Jesus to guard you and your family, protect you, lead you, guide you, and bless you to walk in His Spirit, and follow to know Him. And when the Lord tells you to pray, please pray! You might meet someone to help from a plight that could save their lives.

There was much that happened there in the projects' low-income housing. One night, the Lord woke me and told me to pray for safety, so as I did, there was a drive-by shooting.

Another time I was just home from the hospital where I'd been for dehydration and exhaustion. I was only home a short time when my daughter came running in the house. "Help, mama!"

She and a woman had brought a man, the woman's husband who had been stabbed, into my living room. My daughter was calling

Pastor Johnson, and 911, and the man who stabbed this fellow was pacing the street in a rage. Well, I was praying.

Soon my pastor and assistant pastor were praying at my front door. I know this was overwhelming to my pastor, but it was a way of life to us. I thank the Lord for the men and women of God and their prayers because the Lord had a hedge of protection on my children and me, and a lot of people living there.

As we continued going to the Pentecostal Church, my daughter wanted me to pick up and take children she'd invited to church, so sometimes I would make several trips. And then the Lord directed me to teach Bible studies called, Into His Marvelous Light.

Chapter 6 - Restoration Back to My Real Father

My real father moved close by and had gotten a job, and he was doing well. I asked my pastor if he would give me a prayer cloth anointed with oil and his prayers. I know that through the prayers of my pastor the Lord had blessed that prayer cloth and my father had overcome the addiction of alcohol. He had tried going to some meetings for help, but had not overcome the alcoholic addiction.

After I gave him the prayer cloth, and added my prayers for deliverance, he was able to overcome the addiction. He became a changed man. He worked with my brothers who had an asphalt business. He was hired to deliver parts, and remained strong against any weakness toward drinking. He even came to a play at the church with the children and me.

We would go to his house on Sundays, and after the play, he told JenNel, "If you clean my house, I will pay you." And he told Paul, "If you weed whack or mow the lawn, I will pay you." And he told Joseph, "If you clean my yard, I will pay you." He was teaching them the things I couldn't, because as a single mom of three, I would work to clean house, cook meals, and just be constantly busy paying bills.

After a while, I got close to my real dad. The Lord restored our relationship in my later years, and mended that which was broken. My children and I would visit once a week, and I would bring him a home-cooked meal. And my children would do their chores. He—and we—would enjoy the time we spent together.

My real mom had remarried and I didn't get to see her much. She worked a lot and so did I. We would have BBQ at either one of my brothers' houses on special occasions. Again, we enjoyed and appreciated that family time together.

Loss of a Son

After a short while, my oldest son, Paul, wanted to go visit his father. Pastor Johnson at the time said he didn't know if it was a good choice, but I let him go anyway. What was supposed to only be a summer turned into years, and a lot of that time I didn't know where he was. And then when I finally found him and said, "I want you to come back home," he did, but he was not happy. He wanted to be with his father. When he went back, he took JenNel. She came home after a couple of months, a changed, unhappy teen.

Before leaving, JenNel was faithful to go to church. She won Bible scripture contests and enjoyed going. But she kept insisting. Pastor Johnson wanted to say it was my decision; he remembered when my son went, what was only supposed to be a couple of months turned into years. Even then, I had to threaten my ex for keeping Paul for years and not letting me know where he was (they lived for two years on the side of a mountain). Don had paid one month of child support of $125.

When JenNel came home, she was distant and not happy, and she turned rebellious. There were emotional scars that I could not fix, and she went from a happy young girl who loved her church and friends to a young girl who was troubled. Then, as time went on, the only one she trusted was her grandfather. She fought me. She didn't want to go to church anymore and was very unhappy. Also, she was making friendships with other young women in the projects who didn't go to church.

I was so worn out: I guess I just started to try and figure out what to do on my own. And when I met someone I thought who could fix things, we dated.

Chapter 7 - Not Marrying in God's Will

Pastor Johnson said we could date, just don't fornicate. Well, I was weak and we did.

Andre wanted to marry me then, and I said, "Let's go to the Pastor." He objected. "No, let's just go to the courthouse."

Outside of God's will, I listened to him and we quickly married. But I learned what a womanizer he was.

When you sin, you hide, so we didn't go back to church right away. When we did, Andre announced that we were married. The Pastor had a puzzled look on his face.

I wasn't listening or getting the Word of God in me, but I realized that we were unequally yoked together. Though my children had a good relationship with Andre, now I had two teenagers and a husband who didn't understand about God.

I went to church, but between working, and my family, we weren't faithful to church. We started bouncing around to different churches. It started out okay, but we were not consistent. We would leave that current church and go to another one, then on to another one.

It wasn't working. We were all rebelling and not pursuing after the Lord.

I had a friend who began to come over and want me to do her Sunday School curriculum at Pastor Johnson's church. I knew it was because she was concerned. I was in a backslidden state; how could I help her with Sunday School material when I wasn't doing right?

Chapter 8 - Trying to Climb up Through the Backsliding

One day between the violent movies, two teenagers who were rebellious, and myself following along with them, I saw that my poor youngest son Joseph saw all of this. He would just observe everyone and want to play video games to stay away from the drama. As I grew angrier, I finally turned to God and started praying. I heard the Lord say, You have to tear down images and groves. I was listening, talking to Him, and saying, What is that? He said anything that was displeasing to Him, like bad movies, liquor....

I started walking around the house and getting rid of those things. I took them out and threw them in the dumpster, and the people (neighbors) were diving in for the items. My husband and the kids were getting angrier with me, and I kept telling them that our lives were out of control and we needed to go back to church.

We went to Pastor Bobby Bells in Spring Hill, but only about two or three times. And we weren't reading the Bible or getting a walk with the Lord. We were just attending church, and there is a difference. Our marriage didn't withstand the dividing forces.

The Breakup

Andre had injured his eye at work, so I was driving him to Clearwater five days a week for treatments for several months. As time went on, my car broke down. I told him he had better go to his mom's so he could get a ride. The eye doctor had told him if he didn't get the treatments each day, he could lose his eye. So he walked to the next street to her house.

I didn't see or hear from him after that. He just never came back. As time went by, I sought a divorce. One day there was a knock at the door following an intercessory prayer for Pastor Johnson. It was such deep prayer, but I finally felt a release that it would be okay. But I knew the Enemy was mad when I heard the knock.

It was Andre's ex-wife looking for him. I said, "We are still legally married," and she said she was with him. Then there was a knock on my back door. It was the neighbor that lived behind me, and she was looking for him. She began fighting with his first wife, and I said, "You ladies can take it outside!"

After being married to Andre for over a year, I got the divorce. Sadly, he never returned to church, even after having the influence of a fine Christian family.

Chapter 9 - Failure Over and Over Again

After my second marriage didn't work out, I was working as a cashier. I was informed by some young neighbor woman that my car was in an impound yard…which I had sold to someone who never put it in his name, and I was going to be responsible.

The next thing she said was that my sixteen-year-old daughter, JenNel, was pregnant. I saw the smirk on her face, and I pleaded, "Lord, please remove this young lady."

I asked if someone could take over my money till, and I went home to find this young man there with my daughter. I asked him to leave. Then I called Pastor Johnson.

I turned to JenNel and told her, "I just called the pastor and he said you should marry."

Upon this advice, JenNel married the seventeen-year-old father of her baby. And when Faithe was born, I witnessed a spectacular scene: a rainbow moved across the sheets, and I knew it would be all right.

They got married, but the father, Anthony, was young, and didn't work. Together, we moved from the projects into a singlewide trailer (my father's). But I was the only one working. I had my daughter, her bi-racial husband, and their baby, and my younger son, Joseph, to support.

One day I came home from work. JenNel was tending the baby, but Anthony was just playing video games. Feeling overwhelmed, I told him flatly that they had to move. He sneered, "You won't put us out because of your daughter and granddaughter." We got in a heated argument, and I told him: "Your mom and dad can help you. I can't!"

They left. JenNel was so hurt. I felt such pain at my inability to make things right for her.

They finally moved into an add-on RV trailer because his father wouldn't support him. But one day they fought over an income tax return that he and his sister wanted to squander, while JenNel argued to keep the money for current needs. He drove away with the money. Their marriage didn't work out. After he beat her one night, she came to me with the baby and said she couldn't do it anymore. I said "Fine. I'll help you." And she moved back in with us. After that, the Lord blessed JenNel with a car, and an RV to live in, and she had better times. We had gotten an above ground pool and a gazebo, and she seemed to be a little settled. We had some fun times, and she was a good mom. The ladies at the church I can thank for that, for their prayers.

The Old Trailer

Six weeks apart from each other, my mom and dad passed away. His wish was that my children and I would move out of the low-income housing, into his singlewide trailer. (That was the trailer in which I moved JenNel and her family, along with Joseph.) It was a very old trailer without functional central heat.

Joseph had helped a family move their furniture when they asked him to help, and they gave him two space heaters and only a little money. He was upset, but I tried to tell him that he blessed us by moving them and getting the heaters free, because I wouldn't have been able to buy the heaters. Well, that winter was extremely cold, so it helped more than he knew.

God Moment with a Horse

Joseph saw so much, and I worked a lot. Still, we had things happen that pointed to a loving God.

Through all this, the neighbor had gotten a horse named Summer. One day I was swimming in the pool, and two men came on the land. I said, "Didn't you see the No Trespassing signs?" They said they were from the Census Bureau.

I suspected something, so I said, "Show me your badge." When they didn't have one, I was even more suspicious. I prayed, Lord, send someone to help and protect me.

Suddenly the neighbor's white, beautiful horse came running toward us, and I prayed, If you run these men off, I will let you graze on this land whenever. The horse seemed to know what to do: he galloped toward the men and ran them right off the property. As they ran away, they screamed, "Call your horse off!!"

That horse continued to come every day. The owner would come over with his lasso and tell me how sorry he was. (When I finally told him what happened, he said he couldn't believe it.) The gentle horse would let JenNel hold her daughter Faithe on its back.

The pool became a wonderful family place. One day Joseph put in his little boat that had oars. I told him, "I think it is too big for the pool." While he was paddling, he made a lunge, and suddenly one whole side of the pool dipped and water poured out. Joseph went floating into the neighbor's yard without missing a stride. (I wish I would have had a video camera.) Then he came back laughing and saying, "That was so cool!"

It was pretty amusing, but little Faithe said, "He broke the pool!" "No, we can fill it again," I reassured her.

It was well worth the effort because I saw Joseph smiling and giggling.

We also had enjoyable times on family outings, and with the animals. We would see deer, peacocks, and all sorts of birds. One night my daughter called me to come to her RV. When I got there, a white owl was trying to land on my head. I laughed and said, "I guess I am going to be a wise woman." We all laughed.

Paula Geoghegan

Another Incident of a God-Moment

I was working in a nursing home kitchen, but they weren't going to pay me for two weeks. My lawn needed to be mowed, and I couldn't pay anyone. My thoughts, How could I at least flatten the grass down? I had a piece of paneling leaning on the wall, and I thought I could lay it on the grass and stand on it, and if I heard a noise of a snake, I could just throw a cast iron frying pan given to me, and call on the name of Jesus. I kept doing this around the trailer, and around my car, and toward my daughter's RV on the same property.

Little did I know, my neighbor was watching me, and he yelled, "Hey, lady, aren't you afraid of snakes?"

I said, "They aren't my favorite."

He held his pointed finger to me, and said, "Wait a minute!" He came across my yard with his lawnmower, and I told him I couldn't afford to pay him. He just laughed and said it was free because he never laughed so hard watching a redneck lady in a dress, stomping the grass down, and carrying a frying pan.

He was drinking his beer and mowing my lawn and I was praising the Lord, and his wife came over and she asked me what I said. She said, "He works in the heat, and he doesn't laugh, and now he can't stop laughing!"

When I told her, she, too, was laughing! I made them a nice dinner and thanked them. And they thanked me for entertaining them. Through all that, the Lord saw to getting the lawn mown (by an unlikely but obedient neighbor).

Margaret, the Cashier

I had a friend, Margaret, who was going to her denominational church, and also the Pentecostal church. I had told her to listen for the still, small voice, and to follow His directions.

Margaret and I would go to the home of another friend, Diana, and we would watch Christian movies on Saturday night. One day Margaret called me to tell me she had something for me: mustard seeds. She had gone to the Pentecostal Church, and the

Pastor had preached on a mustard seed of faith. It's all you need, and when you believe, the Lord will work miracles in your situation. I had told Margaret I was asking for an increase of faith because my son was in the service, and confirmed that the Lord speaks of a mustard seed of faith. So she had purchased and brought three packets of mustard seeds, and put them in small containers. She pulled out one mustard seed between her fingers and was rolling it around—but I stuck my whole hand in the container. (As I stated, I wanted an increase of faith.) I felt God would honor the faith I felt. During the time my son Paul was over in Iraq in the army, I came home from working and turned on the news. On the TV, I saw them bringing home young men who had died in the war. Sitting on my couch, I cried and asked the Lord to keep Paul safe.

Suddenly, from the window box air conditioner nearby, something landed on my shoulder. I jumped up from the couch and looked down, and saw a little tree frog. I said, "Why and how did that get through the air conditioner!"

I heard that still small voice…He said, "You did a teaching one time and said FROG meant Fully Rely On God. Are you relying on Me? You are doubting and worrying," And then He reassured me. "Keep praying for Paul, and he will be safe."

I had not heard from Paul for several months and didn't know where he was, and though very concerned, I continued to pray. One day at church, a friend asked about him. When I told her I hadn't heard from him and didn't know where he was, she said, "I work for the government, and I'll take care of it."

Two weeks later, a letter came from Paul, and reassured me he was alright. Pastor Taylor read it to the whole church, and we all rejoiced at the miracle of God's faithfulness.

He did come home safe. Thank you, Jesus.

The following Scriptures were revealed to me as I prayed for Paul's safe return:

Jeremiah 1:5 - "Before I formed thee in the belly I knew thee; and before thou camest forth out of the womb I sanctified thee...."

Luke 12:7 - "But even the very hairs of your head are all numbered. Fear not therefore: ye are of more value than many sparrows.

Jeremiah 29:11 - "For I know the thoughts that I think toward you, saith the Lord, thoughts of peace, and not of evil, to give you an expected end."

Chapter 10 - Too Busy to Know Him

As years went by, I had many jobs: cashier, cleaning motel rooms and houses, and working in a nursing home kitchen. It was very hard trying to raise three children alone. I went to church and tithed my income, but between my job, housework, laundry, and juggling babysitters, I was always tired. I didn't have a prayer life, and I didn't read my Bible. But through all that, Pastor Johnson and the Hudson church family were praying for my children and me.

When I left the projects apartment, I had moved into my dad's trailer. But because it was full of mold, I moved from there into a doublewide.

When I moved to the doublewide trailer, it was roomy and beautiful. But after about a year there, people began breaking into my house when I wasn't there, eating my food, breaking my things, and bullying me. I tried to reach out for help, but was told, "Most people who are stalked by a group of people are terrified to testify," so I endured this. I was getting bitter because of the terror, but I just kept asking the Lord for His help.

A friend bought and put new locks on my door. We changed them three times. I was paying a counselor, but the counselor moved and I couldn't get any help. Then one day I screamed at the top of my lungs that I was going to have them arrested if they didn't leave me alone. They just laughed and mocked me.

This went on for years and I was tired. I had had a heart attack and a stroke from this persecution. Not everyone in the world is nice. Some are cruel and evil. Finally, out of desperation I called upon God and said, "I need Your divine intervention and Your angels to protect me!"

Gradually the persecution lessened, and God continued to help me. (That is why I trust God because no one could help me but God. I chose to heal from the bitterness and to believe one day they have to stand before God for the awful things they did to terrorize me. God will protect and heal from trauma and hurts what people can inflict on you.)

I had heard some quotes from Corrie Ten Boom, author of the book, The Hiding Place. She was a Holocaust survivor and she and her quotes were helping me because I could relate when she said she hated the enemy and was bitter. But then God told her that her bitterness was hurting her, and to forgive so she would be set free. Even though she was being held captive, she was also imprisoned herself because of bitterness. Once she was free, the Lord used her trauma to rescue many from that evil darkness.

During my time at Pastor Johnson's church in Hudson, the Lord had inspired me to teach Bible studies; I used "Into His Marvelous Light" which I had been taught early in my pursuit of God. There were ten students over the course of time, and each one saw and received baptism in Jesus' name. Six received the gift of the Holy Ghost as they heard the Word of God brought to them and saw it for themselves.

Then I had started going to the church where I got baptized, The Upper Room in New Port Richey. Pastor Mark and Becky Huba ministered to me. Sister Huba began to teach me a Bible Study: In My Father's House Home Bible Study. And later I taught "Proclaim the Truth" by Pastor Danny Huba.

Many go to church, but are not in the Word, learning the instructions to living a righteous life. When I was going, I went to church and paid tithes, but at first I did not learn to apply spiritual disciplines like reading and studying the Bible daily. I was missing the key element, His Word. However, the Bible says that faith comes from hearing the Word of God, and as I continued to go, my faith grew and increased under the teaching and personal study of God's Word.

"The Lord looked down from heaven upon the children of

men, to see if there were any that did understand, and seek God" (Psalm 14:2).

"Wherewithal shall a young man cleanse his way? by taking heed thereto according to thy word" (Psalm 119:9).

The word heed means to pay attention, give consideration, or to mind. For when the Lord wants us to read through the Scriptures, we are to listen and believe. His Word speaks to our mind and heart.

"He hath shewed thee, O man, what is good; and what doth the Lord require of thee, but to do justly, and to love mercy, and to walk humbly with thy God?" (Micah 6:8).

"And ye shall seek me, and find me, when ye shall search for me with all your heart." (Jeremiah 29:13).

God's wisdom is infinite. We are not perfect, but we have a perfect God, and He gave us instructions. BIBLE: Basic Instructions Before Leaving Earth.

Even if your family or children are not believers, trust that the Lord can bring them back. The Lord has a banqueting table. It is a blessing and a treasure to be able to go to church, and hear "what thus saith the Word of the Lord" from a man or woman who is anointed to be the Lord's vessel to bring the Word.

Chapter 11 - Surrender

When you finally surrender to God, and totally serve Him, you won't have stunted growth because you'll be in love with your Creator. You will desire to be in His Word. And as you grow in His Word, you will gain knowledge from His Word. As you go to church, obey your preacher as he will have to give an account for your soul one day.

"If the Son therefore shall make you free, ye shall be free indeed" (John 8:36).

"And ye shall know the truth, and the truth shall make you free" (John 8:32).

"Jesus saith unto him, I am the way, the truth, and the life: no man cometh unto the Father, but by me" (John 14:6).

Although the journey has been hard, I will still keep trusting the Lord, for as in John 6:68, we read, "Then Simon Peter answered him, Lord, to whom shall we go? thou hast the words of eternal life."

The victory is when you give your will to the Lord and surrender to His will for your life. I was trying to fill the void of my soul with materialism, or a mate, when the only thing that can fill the void of your soul is the Word of God, loving Jesus, and having a relationship with our Creator.

And now I look back and can blame both my failed marriages on not making the Lord my first love and priority. I followed my mates, and they couldn't lead me in the ways of the Lord. And I couldn't lead them, so in my attempts—because I was not rooted in the Word with a disciplined prayer life and Bible reading and life of study—all I could do was give people my testimony of God's delivering power and saving grace. But if you don't follow on to know Him in an intimate personal relationship, then you are missing the understanding of falling in love with the One who loves you the most. He is the only One who can love you or teach you how to love.

Miracles I Witnessed

I witnessed many miracles which God performed, and want to give Him all the glory. Following is my testimony of those details.

1. When Paul went to Iraq, I didn't know where he was and hadn't heard from him for some time. I was very concerned, praying for his safety every day. A friend at church who worked for the government was able to contact him, and two weeks later she received a letter from him. She gave it to the pastor to read to the congregation, and how we rejoiced!

Paul returned from serving overseas…unharmed! Thank you, Jesus!

2. The baby of one of my brother's was very sick. At the peak of concern, I was holding and rocking the baby, and praying sincerely. Suddenly I heard a strange soft sound like a POP! And I felt the assurance that he was healed, and that his parents would get a good report.

When his parents took him to the next hospital visit, his head had begun to diminish to normal size. Today he leads a normal life, but I know that through various prayer chains, the Lord healed him.

3. Just before making a trip across town with me, Joseph reminded me to pray (it was our routine to do that before driving anywhere). I quickly said, "May 10,000 angels surround us." Joseph wasn't satisfied with the insincere abbreviated prayer rather than our usual sincere one; he said, "That's not the complete prayer we pray, Mom!" But I told him I was tired, that "That should be good enough."

While we were stopped for a turn, a young man rear-ended

us and pushed us a distance, and I ended up in the hospital. My injuries included vertebrae and back damage, and today I am limited in walking short distances, and am unable to drive. It seemed God had to remind me to be steadfast and sincere in my prayers to Him.

However, I was reminded during the accident—I repeated this often—that "I believe it was the angels that kept me. I could hear whooshing sounds" like angels circling me. I'm thankful for a merciful and capable God.

4. My oldest brother had gone to New Jersey to visit our uncle. While my brother shoveled snow, he had a heart attack and was placed in the hospital, but went into a coma. Clinically he died, and the medical staff said he wouldn't make it.

He was still on all the machines when my niece, who had gone to New Jersey for the emergency, called me. She said, "They are not giving him much hope." I felt the Lord had me say, "We walk by faith, not by sight."

Prayer was made, and he survived! Here is how it happened:

I told my niece to ask him to move his finger or wiggle his toes if he could hear her. He moved! She screamed over the phone, "He did move!"

I said, "We are still going to pray, and believe for a miracle." She said, "You've got to come here!" I couldn't get there for another week! But they agreed not to take him off life support. During the week, we continued to pray over the phone, and she would give me updates.

While flying to New Jersey one week later, I had my Bible out, and I asked the Lord for my brother to be sitting up and off life-support. I had seen my mother pass away while on life-support, and I didn't want to see that again.

When the plane landed, my aunt and uncle met me at the airport; I hadn't seen them in over thirty years. They greeted me, and said, "He is awake and sitting up!" They said it was a miracle, and also the doctor said he was a medical wonder.

When I got there, he didn't know who he was, but he was talking and asking questions. We were all amazed. And I knew and my family knew it was only through prayers and the Lord. Thank You, Jesus!

5. A couple of years ago, I got a call in the middle of the night from one of my friends from the projects (Sue) whose son John was in a motorcycle accident. She asked me to come to the hospital. I no longer drove so within twenty minutes my son Paul came. When we got to the Tampa hospital's trauma unit, we learned John needed immediate surgery, but the staff held off because of his condition; they didn't think he would survive in his present state. When I went in, I didn't know what to expect. Sue said with concern, "Someone hit him head on, and he has internal injuries."

When the staff called Sue back, she let her youngest son and me go in. I was more than shocked! John was unrecognizable, and blood was coming from his mouth. I said to the nurse, "May I pray for him?" She encouraged me to pray, saying patients did better after prayer.

That still, small voice had said, Pray for him. When I reached out to find his forehead inside the tremendous swelling of his entire face—all I could identify was his hair—I asked for a miracle, and for the Lord to staunch the blood and take charge of his health care. And as I took my hand off his forehead, my hand rested on his near the siderail bar. I felt his finger slightly tapping mine, and I said, "Jesus is going to help you." It took everything in me to not cry in front of him.

Matt, his younger brother, was very emotional, and anxious. I said, "We are going to believe he'll be okay." Then Matt said to his brother, "John, you're marine strong!

Keep fighting!"

As I left the room, they had a place called the Prayer Garden where people could go to pray for their trauma patients, and I said to Paul and Sue, "Let's go in there." We stood in a circle and prayed. Then we waited. We knew they were having trouble getting the internal bleeding to stop, and that he could go for more surgery if they could stabilize his vitals.

While we were walking to Paul's car, Sue thanked me and I said, "Thank Jesus."

Suddenly John's nurse came screaming out into the parking lot: "The bleeding has stopped!" The signs were looking good for the first time; his vitals were stabilizing and he was showing signs of progress. They would be able to start surgeries.

As we drove home under a sunrise, Paul said, "Mom, I've seen a lot in Iraq, but I know it was traumatic for you." Tears were coming down my cheeks as I continued to pray. Then I heard the Lord speak: In a minute you will see a young man coming around the corner. Watch him. He will be jogging. It's a sign to you that John will recover. The recovery will be a long process, but he'll live.

The jogger came into view, confirming God's message. And two years later at my 60th birthday party at a park, Sue showed me pictures of John standing, and even walking. I cried and she hugged me as she said, "We both know the miracle that God did." John has an awesome testimony of the miracle-working power of the Lord.

"But Jesus beheld them, and said unto them, With men this is impossible; but with God all things are possible" (Matthew 19:26).

6. After I had a stroke, I was using a cane and my body was still wobbly. I asked the Lord that within one month, could He make me whole again without effects from the stroke. Within the month the Lord answered my prayer completely and healed my body. He is worthy of all the glory and honor and praise!

We may question why bad things happen, but I can look back now and say, "I am still here. I may have a disability (from the car wreck), but I am still on the earth…."

I guess the Lord still has me here for a reason, whether it was this testimony or to pray and serve Him as He chooses.

Understanding Salvation

"For I know the thoughts that I think toward you, saith the Lord, thoughts of peace, and not of evil, to give you an expected end" (Jeremiah 29:11).

"In the beginning was the Word, and the Word was with God, and the Word was God" (John 1:1).

"And the Spirit and the bride say, Come. And let him that heareth say, Come. And let him that is athirst come. And whosoever will, let him take the water of life freely" (Revelation 22:17).

Each day Jesus went away alone to pray, to seek instruction from His Father to be able to work the works of healing, teaching, and loving people. And when He was tempted by the devil, He used the Word of God: "It is written…."

The Lord is calling each one of us. Don't silence His still, small voice of invitation. Surrender to His will for your life and ask Him to instruct you in the way of Righteousness. You will be taken on a journey by Him, showing you the gifts and talents He placed in you so you could use them for the kingdom of God. For He knows the plans He has for you, plans to prosper you and to give you a hope and not to harm you and to give you an expected end. The NIV puts it this way:

> "'For I know the plans I have for you,' declares the Lord, 'plans to prosper you and not to harm you, plans to give you a hope and a future'" (Jeremiah 29:11 NIV).

I don't know what has happened in your life, but I know a God who can heal the brokenhearted, set at liberty those who are bruised, and set the captive free. Jesus said He has a free gift. He wants to liberate (free) you.

> "The Spirit of the LORD God is upon me; because the LORD hath anointed me to preach good tidings unto the meek; he hath sent me to bind up the brokenhearted; to proclaim liberty to the captives, and the opening of the prison to them that are bound" (Isaiah 61:1).

He said He would pour out His Spirit upon all flesh. (See Joel 2:28-32.) He has so much for you. All you have to do is be willing and obedient. You have tried many things to fill the void of your soul. Now, how about trying Jesus and His Word? How many friends do you know that gave their life for you? Jesus used Isaiah's prophecy to tell the people of His day the same message:

> "The Spirit of the Lord God is upon me, because he hath anointed me to preach the gospel to the poor; he hath sent me to heal the brokenhearted, to preach deliverance to the captives, and recovering of sight to the blind; to set at liberty them that are bruised" (Luke 4:18).

God has many things to show you as you reach out to Him. He wants to teach you through His Word, things which you do not yet know.

"Call unto me, and I will answer thee, and shew thee great and mighty things, which thou knowest not" (Jeremiah 33:3).

"For God sent not his son into the world to condemn the world; but that the world through him might be saved." (John 3:17)

"For with God nothing shall be impossible." (Luke 1:37).

He is calling you to repentance and full salvation.

"Then Peter said unto them, Repent, and be baptized every one of you in the name of Jesus Christ for the remission of sins, and ye shall receive the gift of the Holy Ghost. For the promise is unto you, and to your children, and to all that are afar off, even as many as the Lord our God shall call. And with many other words did he testify and exhort, saying, Save yourselves from this untoward generation" (Acts 2:38-40).

Pastor Appreciation

I want to express my appreciation to Pastor Mark Huba and his wife, Sister Rebecca Huba. Bishop Huba has giftings of bringing forth the Word of God, and to walk in Wisdom from the Lord. Thank you both for showering me with love and support, and just showing the love of Jesus to me, giving me such a sense of acceptance and love.

I want to thank Pastor Ed Lawson and his family. Pastor Lawson's mother, Sister Caroline, encouraged me to go deeper in prayer. Pastor Lawson was a man of God who also was truly in love with the Word.

To Pastor and Sister Elsworth who were instrumental in praying for me to be guided by the Lord: Thank you. Sister Elsworth prayed and instructed me how to submit to being used of God regarding the gift of Intercession.

I want to give a brief summary of Pastor and Sister Johnson. She was greatly anointed, and a beautiful example of a Godly woman, leading ladies' teas and teachings, bringing the Word of God to light, and teaching us to truly love the Word. Pastor Johnson truly has a deep love to see souls saved and healed, delivered, and rooted in the Word.

To Pastor Bobby Bell (now deceased) and his family, he was truly a man of God who showed the Love of Jesus to my family. He had great insight into the future. At the church he pastored was a beautiful mural of Jesus coming in the clouds. That picture remains as a reminder of Pastor Bell's ministry to me, and his encouragement to "stay faithful."

I want to thank Pastor Dwight and Sister Taylor in pastoring me and bringing forth the Word of God. I especially appreciate Sister Taylor for her precious sweet spirit, and for making me feel special and accepted.

To Pastor Eric and Sister Cristina Sierra, thank you for your desire to see people grow and learn the Word of God. At this current time, Pastor Sierra continues to pastor me through Biblical teaching at The Sanctuary Apostolic Church in New Port Richey, Florida.

I want to give a special thank you for editing this testimony to Sister Peggy Jenkins for her time and kindness to me. She and her husband, Brother Larry Jenkins, are truly a blessing. I thank the Lord for bringing them into my life, and for their disciplined life and true love for souls and for Jesus.

And finally, I want to thank my King Jesus: I thank Him for His mercy and grace, and believing in me. I appreciate and am very honored and blessed to have been privileged for the steadfast love that He gave and has given to me. For His love, wisdom, and patience, I am in amazement and deep gratitude.

And may this testimony bring people to understand that the Lord is calling us to repentance, surrender, and a learning of salvation.

Love always, Your Child, Paula

Chapter 12 - Conclusion

Breaking Down of the Moral Society

Did you know that our Founding Fathers of this Nation were men who feared (honored) God? In historical records is found the following: "It is impossible to rightly govern the world without God" and I would add the Bible. They were praying men, and dedicated the United States and its government under God's direction.

In 1776, the Declaration of Independence was written and approved. In 1787, the Constitution was approved and signed. Yet as years passed, on 1963 June 17, the Supreme Court declared school-sponsored prayer and Bible reading unconstitutional. As we look at the timeframe from then until now, the moral fiber of society has broken down. And what was once held sacred, God's Holy Word was not held in its proper place. Without God's divine Word to lead us in righteousness, men said they would rule. It says in Scripture, "The heart is deceitful above all things, and desperately wicked; who can know it?" (Jeremiah 17:9).

Men obey the laws of the land but have trouble obeying God's laws. There is a hell to shun (avoid), and a Heaven to gain if we love and obey God.

How Diamonds are Made

Did you know that diamonds are made under pressure?

When we see a potter, he uses a lump of clay and while it is on the wheel, the artist crafts and forms a beautiful vase. But sometimes it doesn't form right, so he has to make it over. The Creator of the Universe formed us in our mother's womb for His good pleasure. As we grow, we learn and are shaped but sometimes by wrong choices, poor role models, wrong friendships, hurtful relationships. That can cause heartache, pain, abuse, and leading us to addictions to numb the pain.

Did you know that everything you go through shapes you? And even in trials and heartaches, you can choose to become bitter, or better. We go through life and we make mistakes; we meet friends; we have families; some have jobs with coworkers; some are housewives; some are single parents; some are homeless; some are rich; some are poor, all from different ethnic backgrounds.

We have an invitation to the King; His Name is Jesus. He wants to heal, restore, deliver, and set us free. The Creator of the Universe, God Almighty, knows us by name. He even knows the number of hairs on our head. He looks from His Throne room, and His eyes roam to and fro seeking any who will seek Him. And we all have a story or testimony.

May all that read this book make Jesus Lord and King of their life. And may they learn through a Bible study the importance of baptism in Jesus' name, and the gift of the Holy Ghost.

> "But grow in grace, and in the knowledge of our Lord and Saviour Jesus Christ. To him be glory both now and for ever. Amen" (2 Peter 3:18).

To Him be all the glory and honor. And may you come into the call the Lord has for your life, and to use your gifts, talents, and abilities to work for His Kingdom.

> "Then said Jesus to those Jews which believed on him, If ye continue in my word, then are ye my disciples indeed; And ye shall know the truth, and the truth shall make you free" (John 8:31-32).

This book is written under the Inspiration of the Lord Jesus.

Written by Paula Geoghegan

www.ingramcontent.com/pod-product-compliance
Lightning Source LLC
Chambersburg PA
CBHW060429050426
42449CB00009B/2206